You Are

Author Felisha L. Castoire
Illustrator Valencia Spates

DEDICATION

TO MY BOYS
DAILEN
DOUGLAS
and
DENVER
ALWAYS REMEMBER YOU HAVE GREATNESS WITHIN YOU!

LOVE ALWAYS,

MOM

ACKNOWLEDGMENTS

Thank you to all who have supported and inspired me throughout this journey.

Joe was having a terrible week in school. It was his third day in a new school, and today was the worst day of them all for him. He couldn't seem to make new friends. He was sure everyone would like him; after all he was very unique. Unfortunately for Joe, things turned out differently every time he tried.

Joe arrived home from school in a somber mood. He wanted to ask his mother an important question but didn't know how. Joe's Mom noticed his mood and decided to have a talk with him that evening.

"Joe, it's time for your bath then it's off to bed." said Joe's mom.

"Awe Mom! Okay." Joe replied.

"Mom, can I ask you something?" asked Joe

"Sure Joe." Joe's mom responded.

"Would you be my friend if you were my age?" asked Joe. "Am I different?"

"Joe, there are a few things I want you to always remember." said Joe's mom.

"A few things to remember?" asked Joe. "Like what Mom?"

"Always remember you are this whole being; that is true." said Joe's mom. "You are filled with wonderful qualities that make up you."

"A whole being?" asked Joe "I am?"

"Yes, you are! replied Joe's mom. "You are full of laughter, love, charisma and charm."

"I do like to laugh," said Joe. "but sometimes Sam in my class says that he does not like me because I'm not cool enough.

"Yes, you are cool and likeable!" said Joe's mom. "You are filled with intelligent thoughts that can do no harm."

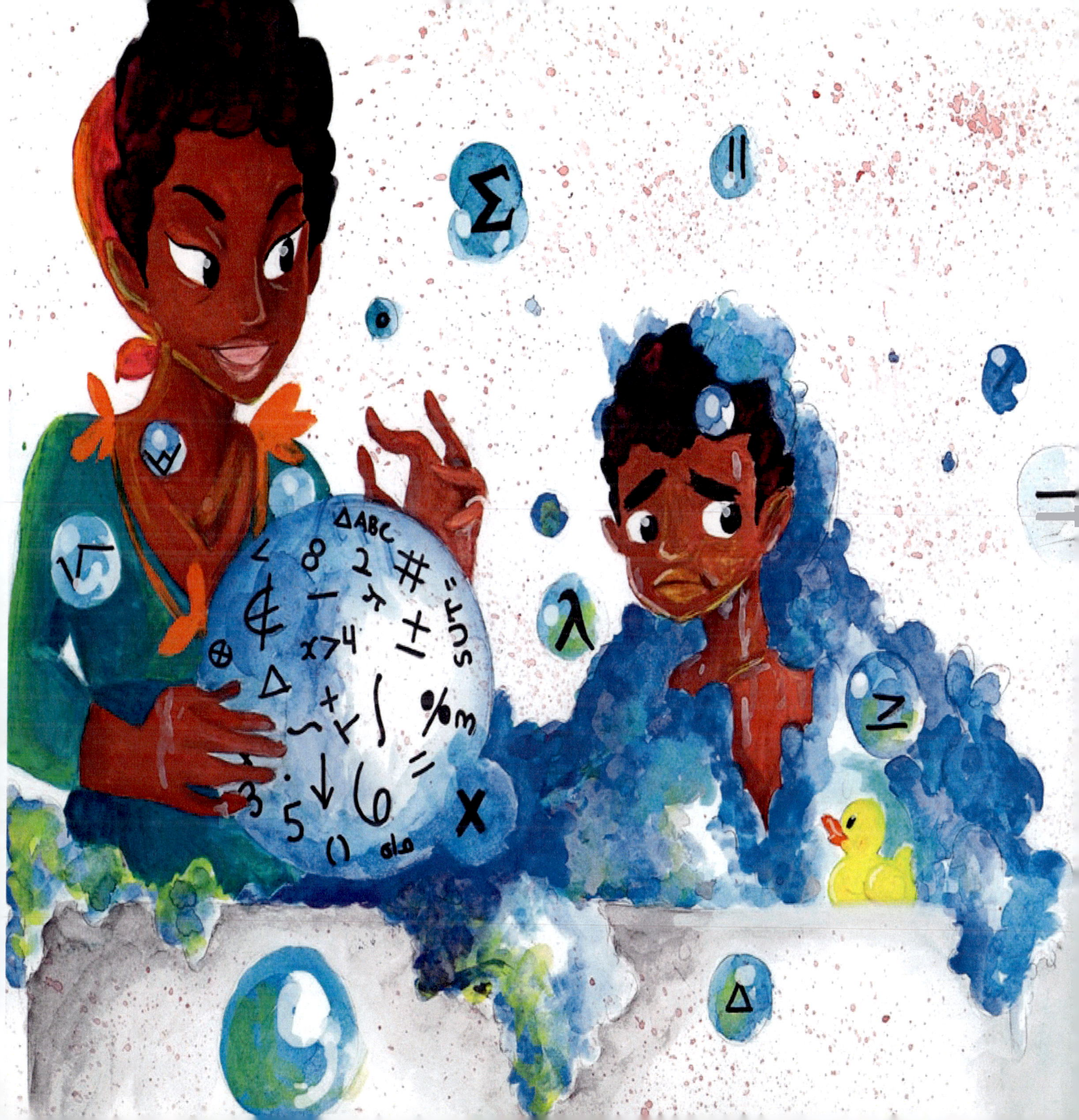
ΔABC

"Even if Christopher R. at tutoring says I'm not?" questioned Joe.

"Yes, you are intelligent!" exclaimed Joe's mom.

"Wait, I did get a 95% on my last spelling test! I am smart! Joe proclaimed.

"You are a person with a caring heart and a beautiful smile." said Joe's mom.

"Even if some of the girls call me gross?" asked Joe.

"Yes, you are Joe." Joe's mom reassured him.

"You are handsome and kind and it makes being in your presence always worthwhile."

"I do look really nice when I put on my lucky bow tie," said Joe "and wearing it makes me feel good." "You know, I am handsome!"

"Yes, you are!" said Joe's mom.

"I am? Joe asked "Even if big cousin Mark calls me a weirdo?"

"Yes, you are valuable and unique!" replied Joe's mom. "You are this whole being that is true! Yes, this whole being that is you!"

"I am! Aren't I?" pondered Joe.

"Yes, you are!" replied Joe's mom.
"You are courageous and strong with a great imagination."

"Even if the kids on the playground call me shrimpy?" inquired Joe.

"Yes Joe, you are strong." declared Joe's mom.

"Well, at recess I can hang from the monkey bars longer than all the other kids." Remembered Joe "Wow, I am strong." Realized Joe.

"You are very clever and bright with a strong desire to learn." encouraged Joe's mom. "You are one of our greatest creations."

"I am clever. I do tell the best jokes!" laughed Joe.

"Mom, sometimes I take a long time doing my homework." "Am I still smart? questioned Joe.

"Yes, you are!" answered Joe's mom."

"I take a long time because I want ot make sure it's correct." Explained Joe. "Yes, I am a bright kid." Decided Joe.

"Your energy is amazing." she continued "Your enthusiasm is unmatched. Your bravery and love keep my heart attached."

"Hey Mom, I know I'm brave. I'm not even afraid of the dark or bugs! Joe exclaimed. "I sound pretty amazing!"

"Because you are." said Joe's mom with a smile.

"I'm an awesome, amazing, and super fantastic kid! Joe shouted.

"Yes, you are." beamed Joe's mom.

"Every day people will say things about you, some good and some bad. What matters the most is what you believe to be true." explained Joe's mom. "It is important to believe in all the great qualities you possess. Knowing your worth will lead you to success."

"You are this whole being that is true full of great qualities and I love you!" professed Joe's mom.

"Hey, Mom?" Joe asked with a quizzical look on his face.

"Yes Joe." said his mother.

"That was more than a few things to remember, but I can do it!" beamed Joe.

Circle all your great qualities

Honest	Cheerful	Forgiving
Gentle	Smart	Trusting
Reliable	Kind	Helpful
Clean	Athletic	Generous
Energetic	Ambitious	Respectful
Responsible	Wise	Thoughtful
Confident	Adventurous	Outspoken
Fearless	Persuasive	Patient
Energetic	Strong	Attentive
Independent	Courteous	Funny
Mature	Interesting	Appreciative
Joyful	Listener	Talkative
Polite	Disciplined	Courageous
Empathetic	Curious	Fair
Brave	Sincere	Happy

Fill in the blanks using the words above

I am_____, _____, and

_____. I am proud to be me

Questions

1. What were the challenges Joe faced at his new school?

_____

2. Joe's mother offered him words of encouragement, what advice would you give Joe?

_____

3. Have you ever experienced someone calling you a bad name?

_____

4. How did it make you feel?

_____

5. Joe had to remind himself of all his great qualities, why was that important?

_____

6. What are some of your great qualities?

_____

7. When faced with a challenge how does that make you feel? Do you give up or keep trying? Why?

_____

_____

HOW TO ENHANCE YOUR SELF-ESTEEM

The way we feel about ourselves has a huge affect on the way we treat ourselves and others, and on the kinds of choices we make. Here are some things you can do to protect, raise, or reinforce your self-esteem.

- Spend time with people who like you and care about you.
- Ignore (and stay away from) people who put you down or treat you badly.
- Do things that you enjoy or that make you feel good.
- Do things you are good at.
- Reward yourself for your successes.
- Develop your talents.
- Be your own best friend - treat yourself well and do things that are good for you.
- Make good choices for yourself, and don't let others make your choices for you.
- Take responsibility for yourself, your choices, and your actions.
- Always do what you believe is right.
- Be true to yourself and your values.
- Respect other people and treat them right.
- Set goals and work to achieve them

YOU ARE

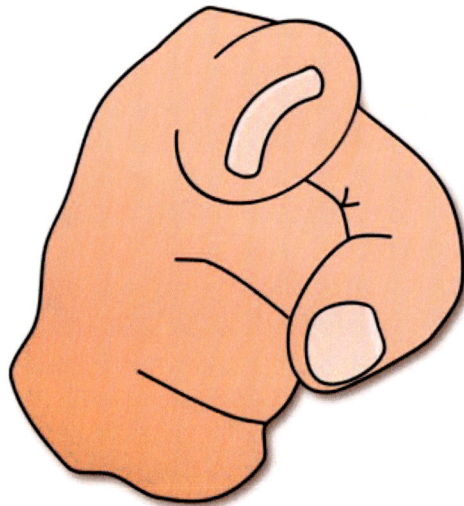

AMAZING!

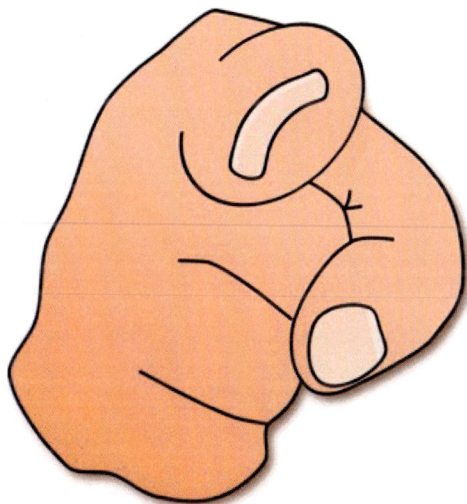

FLC123LLC

ABOUT THE AUTHOR

Felisha L. Castoire was born and raised in Staten Island, NY. She is the owner of her own family daycare and the mother of three wonderful boys. Felisha took the advice she gives to her children and the children she cares for and put them into stories, allowing her message of encouragement and self-empowerment to be read by all children.

To contact author

www.123flc.com

www.facebook.com/youarejoe

Twitter/Instagram

fabfeesh

FLC123LLC